Multiracial

Jason Wh

THE ENGLISH CENTRE
EBURY TEACHERS CENTRE
SUTHERLAND STREET,
S.W.1.

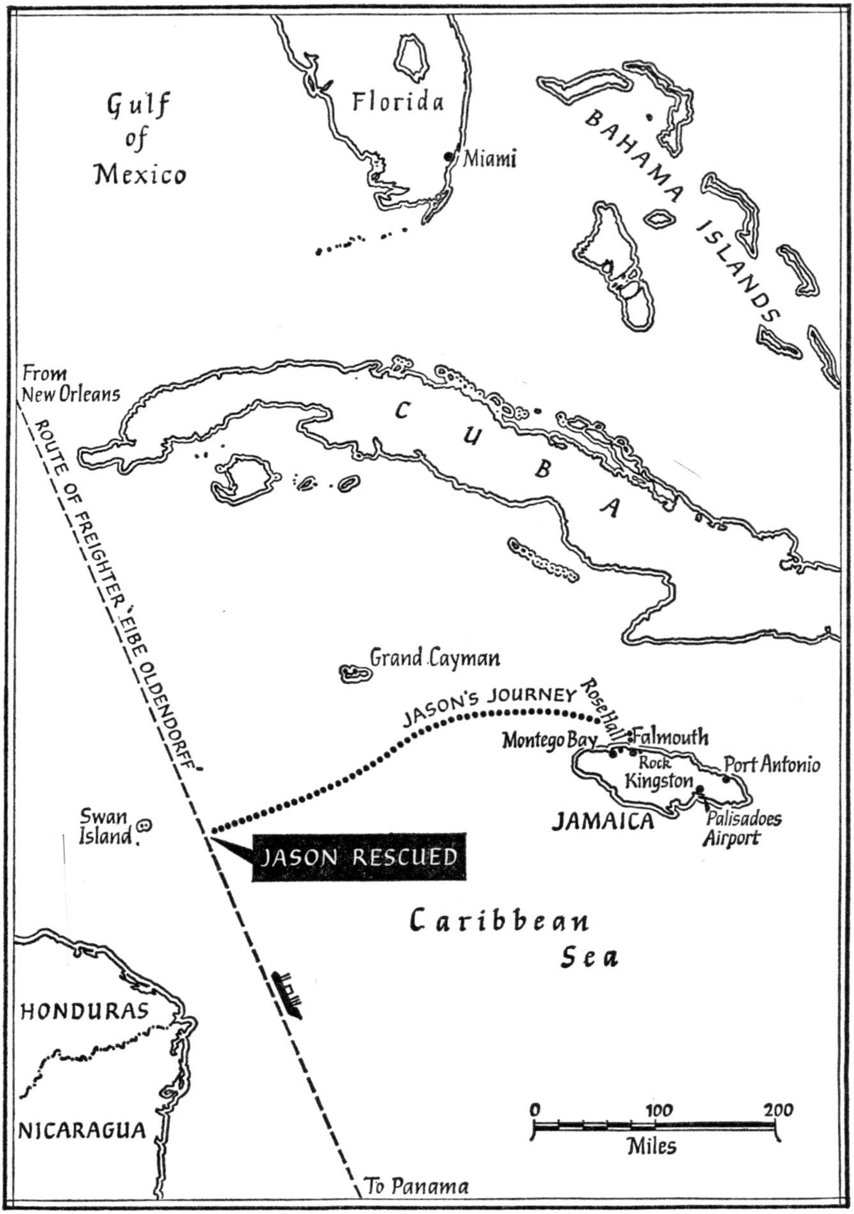
Gulf of Mexico
Florida
Miami
BAHAMA ISLANDS
From New Orleans
C U B A
ROUTE OF FREIGHTER 'EIBE OLDENDORFF'
Grand Cayman
JASON'S JOURNEY
Rose Hall
Montego Bay
Falmouth
Rock
Kingston
Port Antonio
JAMAICA
Palisadoes Airport
Swan Island
JASON RESCUED
Caribbean Sea
HONDURAS
NICARAGUA
0
100
200
Miles
To Panama

Jason Whyte, Jamaican
TERRY PARRIS

Illustrated by Trevor Stubley

LONDON
OXFORD UNIVERSITY PRESS
1973

For Jason and the children of Jamaica

*This is a true story.
I have been privileged to tell it.*
                        TERRY PARRIS

Contents

		page
1	Jason at home	7
2	The fishing trip begins	10
3	Jason and his father try to turn back	14
4	The lights of home	17
5	Drifting	21
6	The open sea	24
7	Rough weather	27
8	Jason and a dolphin	31
9	Jason alone	35
10	The rescue	39
	Questions	44
	Glossary	46

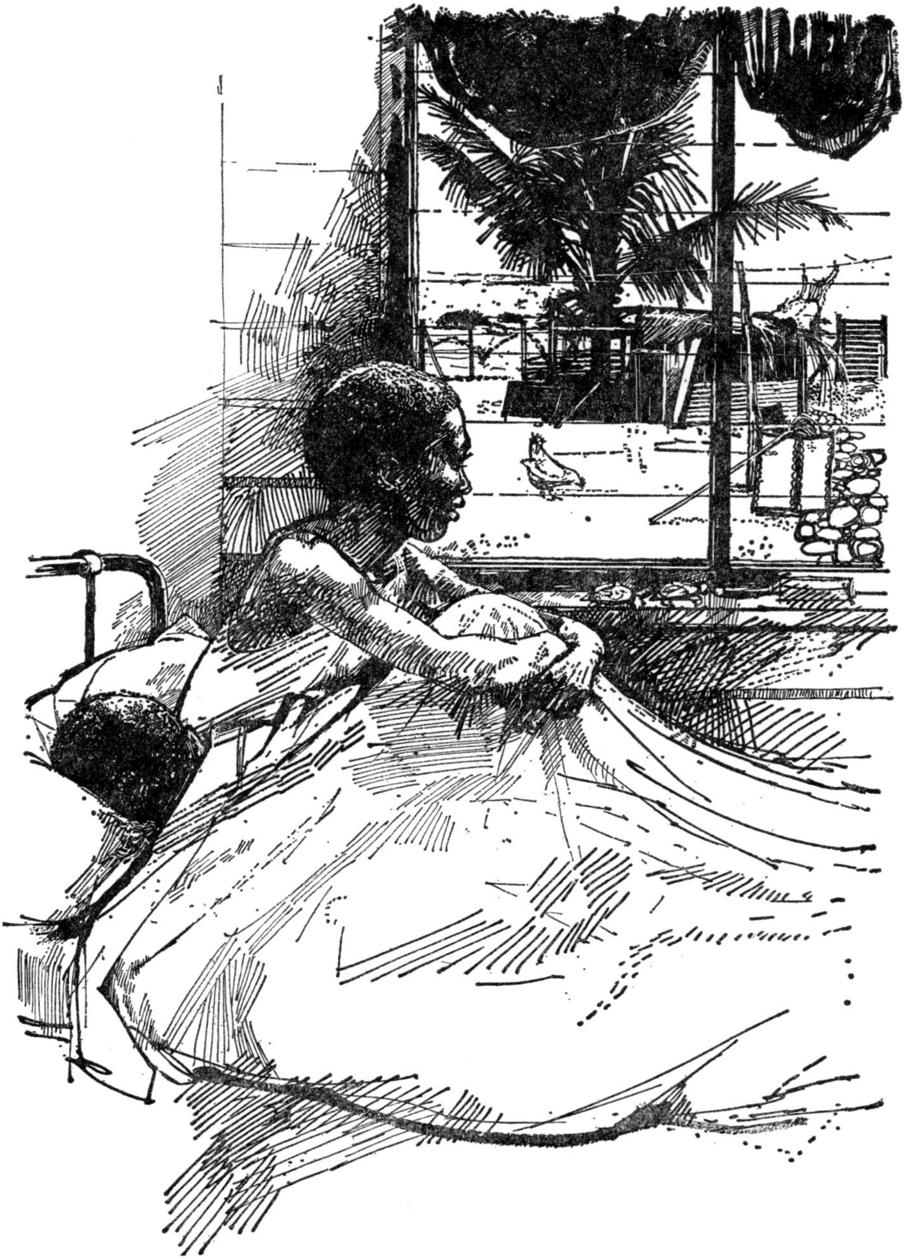

1. Jason at home

When Jason woke up he felt happy. It was Saturday. He could do all the things that he liked to do most.

'I shall carve,' he thought to himself. 'I shall carve little turtles to sell to the tourists. I shall sit in the yard and carve. Then I'll go to see my grown-up friend, Mr Hector Thomas. He is like me. He works alone. But he doesn't mind having me with him. He will let me help while he makes tables and chairs.'

Jason and Mr Thomas had spent many silent hours together, while the boy watched the man at work. Jason thought that he might like to be a cabinet-maker when he grew up.

Jason stretched himself on the narrow bed. He could feel the warmth from his young brother, Albert. He looked at Albert's sleeping face. 'Albert is dreaming, far away,' he thought. 'But when Albert is awake his eyes shine, and he laughs and talks all the time.'

A rooster crowed in the yard. Jason sat up and looked out of the window. He could smell the strong smell of the mangrove swamps. The coconut tree was still there and so was the bright yellow marl. One day the marl would be beaten flat to make more land for building. Meanwhile it stood up like peaks of golden sand.

"I wonder where the sea birds will go when the swamps are all filled in with marl," Jason said aloud.

He turned his head away from the window. He looked at his big sister Daphne and her children, little Marcia and Richard, all asleep in the double bed.

"Daphne shouts when the children bring in marl on their feet," he said, "but she says that marl is good. It will give us more land for building."

"I am Albert Whyte," said Jason's brother in his sleep. "I go to Falmouth All Age School, and I like English, History and Geography."

Jason hugged his knees under the cotton sheet, and smiled. He thought, 'Albert is still dreaming! Even in his dreams he talks!'

"You like to talk like Papa," he whispered, "and you have many friends. Papa has a lot of friends, too."

Jason lay down again. A smell of frying fish came in through the window. The big, fat, black pig was grunting as she hunted in the garbage can. He heard Sister Sarah's little girl, Cassandra, crying for her breakfast. He decided that he would get up to have some porridge and fried fish, too. He rolled quietly out of bed and put on his old pair of khaki pants. 'No fresh pants or clean khaki shirt today,' he thought. 'You can stay in the drawer till Monday!'

Mama was cooking on the kerosene oil stove outside. She looked very big and tall as she turned the fish with one hand while stirring the porridge with the other. Jason couldn't remember ever seeing Mama without children around her. She had nine daughters: Jason's sisters. And all were older than he was. Except for nineteen-year-old Rhona, all of them now had children of their own. 'Children and grandchildren,' Jason thought. 'Mama has plenty of grandchildren.'

"Princess, Herma, Charmian, Cassandra . . . come," called Jason's mother. "Eat your porridge."

Jason sat quietly on the verandah wall and swung his legs. He watched Princess help Sarah's baby, Cassandra, with the porridge. Cassandra ate very fast. Princess hardly had time to dip the spoon back into the bowl!

Jason hoped that Mama had put some food on one side for Sister Daphne, and for Marcia and Richard. He could remember when all the family were crowded into the old house down the road. Now they had three rooms. He had watched his father show the carpenter how the wooden house should be built. That had been eight years ago, when Jason was six years old.

"Where's Papa?" Jason asked his mother now.

Mama poured more oil into the pan. Then she began to cut up some plantains. She never used many words.

"Gone to Falmouth," she said, "to buy gas."

The joy of Saturday was gone. 'No carving after all!' he thought. 'Fishing instead. I wanted to carve.'

"Papa said last week that he was getting too old to fish. He said he wasn't going fishing any more. The outboard motor isn't working."

"It's mended," said Mama briefly. "You and Papa are going fishing. But not until the afternoon. You can spend the morning carving."

2. The fishing trip begins

The brown and white boat was home to Jason. The house was a place to sleep in. The yard was a place to work in. But the boat was a place to live in.

"I have been carving turtles all the morning," said Jason aloud, as he ran down to the sea. "The tourist bus comes to Fisherman's Inn tomorrow. Then, if I am lucky, the tourists will give me a dollar each for the carvings. It would have been good to stay in the yard. It would have been good to help my friend, Mr Hector Thomas, too. But when Mama says I must go fishing—I must go fishing!"

Jason knew every inch of the boat. It was only two months since he had painted it. The lettering of its name stood out clearly: WHAT'S THAT TO YOU?. The name was a challenge. His father liked challenges. Papa liked to throw out challenges to everyone. He always enjoyed a good argument with his friends.

Jason jumped into the boat, and started the engine. The water had been cool on his feet after the hot shore. Now the boards of the boat felt warm and friendly. His brown toes curled round the one paddle lying in the bottom. The line to catch fish was there, and so was the gaff: the stick with the iron hook on the end which was used to pull the fish into the boat.

"Perhaps this is better than carving, old boat," said Jason. "You and Papa and I go well together. What shall we catch today? Our friends in the deep sea are waiting for us. Shall it be albacore, bonito, dolphin or kingfish? They all sell well in the market."

It was only a mile to Falmouth from the few houses in Rock village, where Jason lived. Jason kept close to the shore. He steered the boat with one hand and trailed the other through the clear blue-green sea. He saw starfish, looking like giants on the sandy bottom. He saw salmon-pink conch shells, and brown ones, and green weed waving with the motion of the water. The motor chugged steadily as the houses of Falmouth began to appear. Some of the houses looked very old, with wrought iron balconies. Papa had told him that once, long ago, Falmouth was in the richest sugar area in Jamaica. As the harbour came nearer Jason wondered what it had looked like then, when it was full of ships, all being loaded with sugar. When Papa was a very young man he had worked at the harbour, helping to load the sugar.

"I can remember Papa only as a fisherman," Jason said to the boat. "He has been going out for two or three hour trips, several times a week, for as long as I can think back."

Papa was not alone when Jason reached Falmouth. He seldom was alone. As he stowed the tin of gasolene under the cover, he pointed to another boat, a canoe like his own, bobbing gently near by. There were three men in it, whom Jason knew well.

"Our usual friends," Papa chuckled in his deep voice. "Have you met my son, Jason, masters? Jason, this is Special Constable Charley Dennis, Mr Henry, and 'Reds'."

The three men laughed at Mr Whyte's joke. They had known Jason since he was a baby.

"What happened, Jason?" one said. "Why is it that you have so many sisters? Don't you and Albert have a hard time with those women in the family?"

Jason did not answer. He knew the men very well. They often went fishing together. He liked to talk to himself when he was alone, but he was very quiet with others. He started up the engine, and listened to his father shouting across to the other men. As the boats went farther and farther out to sea, the blue of the water deepened. The sun went lower in the sky.

Papa was trailing the line behind the boat. "Three hours of work, and we'll be back home with a fine haul," he said. But just at that moment the motor spluttered, and then stopped.

3. Jason and his father try to turn back

Papa looked round at the sea and the sky.

"The sky's clear, and the sea's calm," he said. "No hurry, Jason. We'll soon have the motor going again."

As Jason took the cover from the tank he saw Papa glance at the boat with his friends in it, and smile. He waved, and they waved back. Jason worked the motor, and tried to get it started. It gave a cough, almost started, and then stopped.

'I expect there is water in the gas-tank,' Jason thought. 'But at least we have another full tin of gas.' The engine started, coughed, and stopped again. Jason stopped trying for a moment and looked deep into the water. It was still clear, and a Portuguese man-o'-war floated by, slowly waving its tentacles. Branches of coral shone in the deep water, and when Jason leant right over the side of the canoe he could see small golden and white fish darting busily this way and that.

"Dreaming again, man?" laughed the boy's father. "The sun's going down, and this won't get us home!"

Jason loved his father's laugh. Papa was an old man now, but he was a gay, strong man still. Everyone was happy when Papa was around.

Now the boy tried the motor again with the fresh tin of gas, and it started. It started, and it went on going.

"We're going back," Papa shouted to his friends. "I don't trust this outboard, Charley!"

"Cho' man," shouted Charley. "We want to get the big fish. See those flying fish? There must be big fish around here following them!"

"They'll be here tomorrow," said Papa. "I'm getting too old for this game!"

"Reds" stood up in the stern of their boat. He liked William Whyte. "We're going on," he shouted. "You come too!"

"They can go on," Jason's father said to himself. "I never really wanted to come fishing today."

"You haven't been feeling too well, Papa?" asked Jason.

William Whyte did not answer. 'Perhaps he didn't hear,' thought Jason. The old man was watching the line trailing behind. The boat went steadily towards the shore. Although they were still far out, Jason could see the tree-lined beaches faintly in the distance. Behind him, the huge sky was golden in the setting sun. Now he could feel the evening breeze blowing from the shore.

"I was going to send you fishing today with a friend of mine," said William Whyte. He laughed, and looked fondly at his son. "But I changed my mind!" The line pulled on his gnarled hand, but it was only weed, and he took it off.

"Your Mama will be pleased to see us," he said. "She's a fine woman, your mother. We've been together a long time now. A quiet, good woman; no fussing with her."

Jason felt proud to hear his father speak that way. He said nothing, but he felt proud. He turned his head away to hide his feelings, and looked at the dark line of the horizon.

The motor stopped.

"Water in the carburettor again," said William Whyte. "I'll soon get it going."

But again the outboard motor refused to start. Jason's father tried. Jason tried. They tried together. The only sound was the lapping of the water against the sides of the boat.

"Charley! Reds!" Mr Whyte shouted. "The motor's died! Charley, can't you hear?"

The sun was almost down to the water-line. A golden path flowed from it to their boat. Jason could see the other boat clearly in the distance, dark against the same golden light. Mr Whyte stood up to call.

"Hey, man . . . come! The motor has died, man!" He turned to Jason. "They don't seem to hear me."

"Mr Henry!" Jason shouted. "Mr Dennis! Mr Dennis!"

The sea heaved gently in the golden light. The other boat went up and down in the slight swell. Jason did not know why they sat, unmoving, unhearing, in the other boat.

4. The lights of home

"They're too far away to hear," said Jason's father at last. "They can't hear if their motor is going, anyway. Let's stop calling, and start to paddle. I'll take the first turn."

As his Papa took up the one old paddle, Jason pulled the line in. It was best to think about getting home now. He put the line in the bottom of the canoe under the spare boards, and trailed his hand through the water. He noticed the speed of the water against his hand. He watched the sun go down into the ocean. The land breeze was very cool.

"The westward current is strong," said Jason's father. He looked at the dark water as it swirled by the paddle. "I think it will be better for us when the moon comes up. It will be a moonshine night, I know."

Jason idly caught pieces of weed drifting by. 'It looks rather like love-bush,' he thought. The yellow-orange love-bush grew all over the bushes near their house. His grown-up friend, Mr Hector Thomas, had told him that if you planted a piece and it grew, it meant that the person you loved, loved you. Jason smiled in the darkness to himself. It was foolishness, he thought, but nice foolishness. "Mr Thomas is a nice man," he said to himself. "And he is my special friend." He threw the dripping weed back into the water.

"Your turn, man," said his father. "Are you sitting dreaming?"

Papa's voice was deep and warm, thought Jason. Warm, like the sun on rocks. The sea was different. It was cold, especially here, where the water was deep. But soon they would be on the 'shelf' and near to shore; it was good to think of the shelf running round the island. Jason thought that he would like to be a sea bird, and look down on the sea from a great height.

17

Then he would see the shallow part, the shelf, and know where the steep drop of the ocean bed began.

Jason's father put the paddle into his hand. Jason felt the rough wood like a friend.

"You're like your mother, boy. You don't talk much!" the old man laughed.

"You don't talk much at sea, Papa," said Jason, as he dipped the blade of the paddle into the water.

William Whyte laughed again.

"You mean not as much as I do on land!" he said. "Fishermen don't talk at sea."

The moon was coming up as Jason started paddling. The dark water changed to a steel-grey. The first stars appeared. Jason felt sure that they were getting nearer to land. He could see the dark shape of his father in the bow. The shape was drooping, and Jason remembered that his father was sixty-eight.

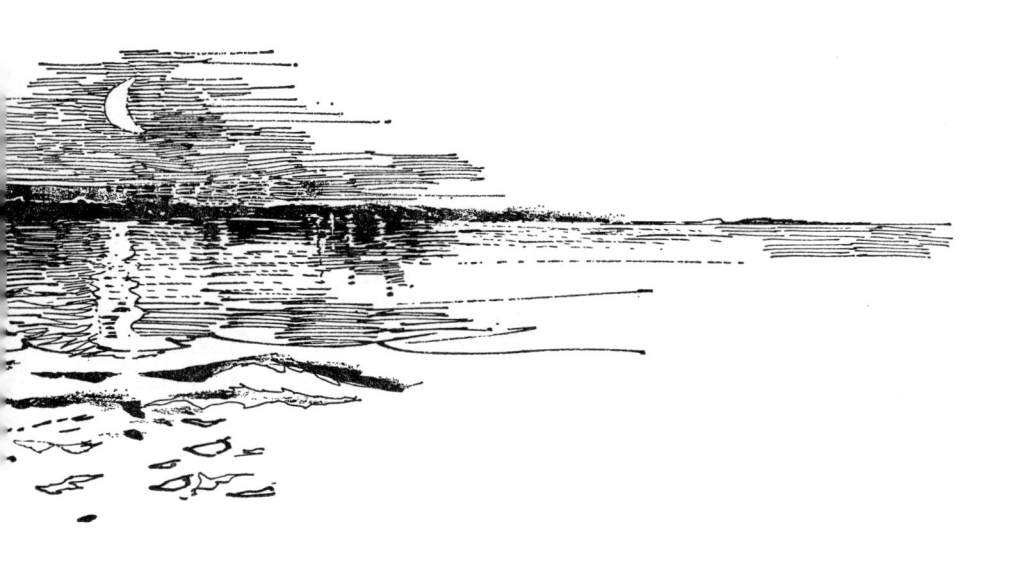

It was hard to remember, because Papa was so strong and active. The boat moved smoothly through the water.

"Is it going well, man?" Papa asked. "I can never go very fast with one paddle."

"It is going well, Papa," said Jason.

He paddled evenly, hardly making a splash. Sometimes the water shone like silver as the paddle moved through it. Jason thought of the lagoon near his home, where all the tourists came at night. There the water shimmered and glistened. It was very beautiful. Jason dreamed, but soon his back began to hurt, and the palms of his hands began to feel sore.

"There are some lights on the shore." His father spoke suddenly, and excitedly. "We're not lost, man. They're lights."

Jason knew those lights. They were the lights of the Holiday Inn Hotel at Rose Hall. He had seen them often. He was pleased, but surprised to know that Papa had thought they might be lost. Jason had never thought they were lost. He handed the paddle to his father.

William Whyte paddled fast. He forgot that it had seemed hard before. He put all his strength into the stroke. It was strange then, he thought, that the lights still looked as far away as before.

"You've done enough, Papa," said Jason. "It's my turn now."

Jason paddled in silence. He shared the puzzlement of his father. It seemed that as they moved four feet forwards, the land breeze blew them six feet backwards. Jason's palms burned like fire. He pulled the paddle into the boat. Suddenly, he was asleep.

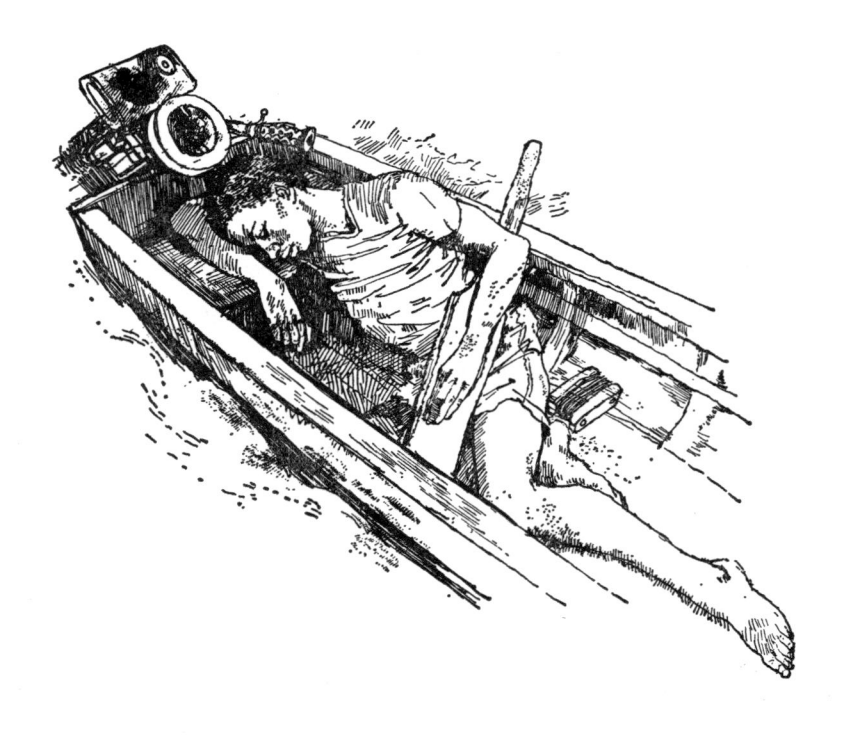

5. Drifting

It was cold when Jason woke up, and he could not think where he was. He stretched out a hand in search of his sleeping brother Albert, but his hand touched wooden boards instead.

"What's that?" mumbled a voice near his feet. "What did you say?"

Jason opened his eyes and looked around. He seemed to be lying in the bow of his father's canoe. Why was he here, and not in his bed with Albert? And where was his father? He sat up. He was at sea with Papa. His father was half asleep in the stern. The paddle lay between them. The canoe was drifting. 'Now I remember,' he thought. 'We were going home. I went off to sleep before I reached the shore. Papa must have gone to sleep too. We were so tired. Where are we now?' He looked towards the shore.

The fresh green shore was there, but far, far away. Jason could only just see the white line of the surf. They must be as far out to sea as they had been last evening, before they had started to paddle. It was the hour before daylight. Jason put his hands on the wooden side of the canoe to warm them. In the half light, the water looked deep, cold, and blue. He could see where it changed to green far away, closer to the shore. The mass of clouds on the horizon became slowly lighter. Jason could see the golden light creeping upwards. He felt hungry.

Mr Whyte sat up slowly.

"Why is my back so stiff?" he asked. "Where are we, Jason?"

"We've been asleep all night," said Jason. "We've drifted back out to sea."

William Whyte pushed himself up on to the wooden seat. He watched the edge of the sun as it rose from the water-line.

"The current has taken us westwards," he said. "We must be past Montego Bay."

The sea was calm. It was flat and dead still. Jason handed the fishing line to his father, and started to paddle. He felt hungry, but he was fresh with the rising sun, and a new day was beginning. The shore looked a long way away.

"Now, if we could catch a dolphin," said Jason's Papa, "we could cut it up and use it for bait. A big jack-fish or a snapper would make a fine breakfast!"

Jason smiled to himself as he paddled. Papa always liked his fish steamed, with a snowy pile of rice beside it. He must be mad to talk of eating raw fish. But if he could catch a fish, Jason thought, it would be good for Mama to cook. Then Jason wondered how long it would take to reach Rock. The distant shore in front of them must be some other part of the coast.

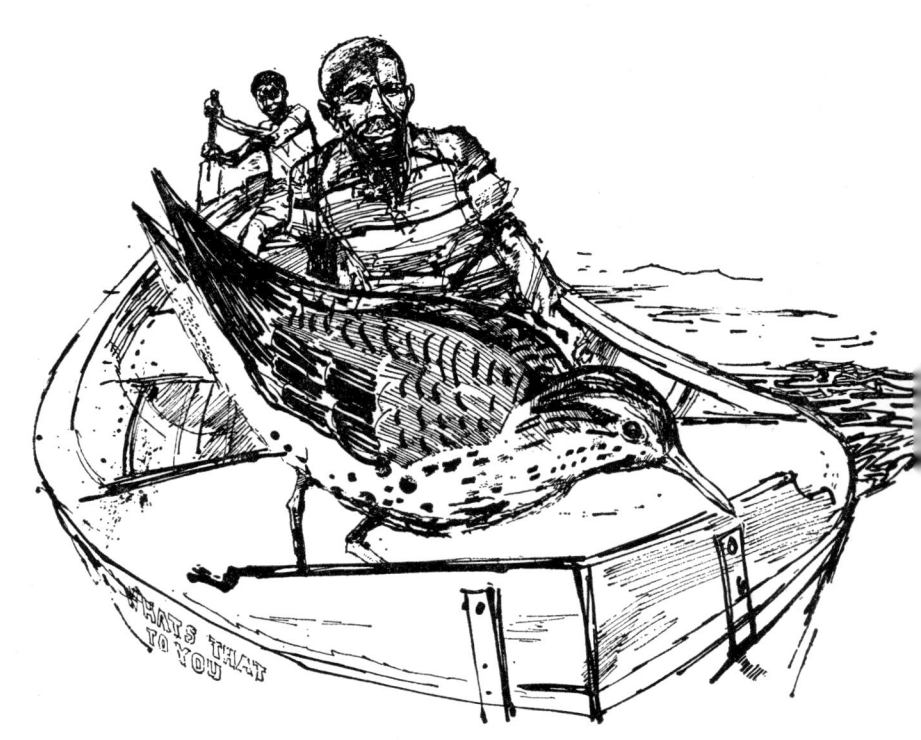

The sun was climbing higher in the sky. A small brown and white bird flew low towards them and landed for a moment on the end of the boat near Jason's father. Jason thought that it might mean that they were getting nearer land. He had seen birds like it in the mangrove swamps. Jason liked to climb among the snaky roots of the trees, and push his toes into the black mud.

"No fish biting yet," said William Whyte, "but that was a friendly bird. I wonder if your mother sent him, eh, Jason? Have a rest, man. Your Mama will have reported us missing by now. Yes, she'll have said we haven't come back. They'll send out a search party for us soon. Rest, man. We'll watch for a little aeroplane, or a motor-launch."

Jason could see that his father was uneasy. He pulled in the paddle, and looked round. The sun was warm, and there was a light breeze. But the shore did not seem any nearer.

"Give me the paddle, and I'll work for a while," said William Whyte. "Man, but I'm hungry!"

The clouds had all gone from the sky. It was a deep blue. 'Not a sign of an aeroplane,' thought Jason. 'Nor of a helicopter, either.' It would be exciting to be picked up by a helicopter, or even a motor-launch! Albert would love it. He could tell all his friends at school on Monday, "My brother Jason was rescued by a motor-launch!"

Jason lay down. The sun was burning his back.

"People will come searching soon," William Whyte repeated. "They'll find us today."

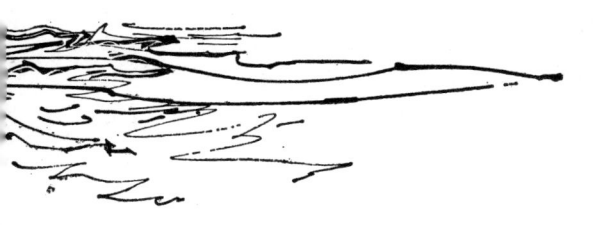

6. The open sea

"I was wrong," said William Whyte the next morning. "They didn't find us. But they will today. A little boat on this great open sea. It will be easy to see us."

Jason did not speak. He looked round at the blue water. That was all there was. No land in sight at all. It seemed useless to use the paddle. He didn't know where the island lay. 'I'm not sure,' he thought, 'that Papa's right about an aeroplane spotting us.' When his big sister, Sister Sarah, had gone to Canada to work, she had written them a letter telling them about her flight in the aeroplane. She had said that from a great height all you could see was the white heads of the waves. But perhaps the aeroplane looking for their boat would fly very low, thought Jason. How would it know that they had drifted so far away, though? They must be hundreds of miles from Jamaica by now.

"The sun's fierce today," said William Whyte. "We ought to have brought a bottle of water."

Jason felt very thirsty himself. He dared not think about water. His tongue felt big and dry in his mouth. He tried a handful of salt water, but it made him feel sick.

"Shelter under the cover," Jason's Papa said. "You look hot, man." Sweat was running down the backs of his own legs, and it trickled down the side of his face. 'I'm hungry,' William Whyte thought. 'I hope the boy is not as hungry as I am.' He looked at the sea all around, and felt very much alone.

"I'll say a prayer," he said.

Jason looked at his feet and listened.

"Dear Father," said Mr Whyte. "You know that Jason and I are lost at sea. We are in your hands, dear Father. Please send someone to come and rescue us."

Jason, listening, felt strangely comforted. He looked at his father, who was still praying in a low voice. Jason felt how much he loved his father. The deep voice stopped, and there was a long silence.

"No man is ever alone," Mr Whyte said suddenly.

"I'll try the motor again," Jason said. He came out into the hot sun. He worked carefully on the motor, cleaning out the carburettor. It still wouldn't start. 'I must do something,' he thought. 'I'm hot, and the motor won't start. I'll swim!' Jason jumped into the water

"Hey, man," shouted his father, "what are you doing?"

"Swimming!" shouted Jason. "You should come in!"

He was happy. The water was warm, but much cooler than the sun on his back. He dived, and came up; dived again, and circled round the boat. His father laughed to see him shake the drops of water from his dark head. Jason laughed too, and forgot where they were; forgot that they had no food and water.

"Listen!" Jason shouted suddenly. "Can you hear that? I'm coming in."

He swam to the side of the boat, and his father helped him to scramble in.

"It's an aeroplane," he said excitedly. "There, high up in the sky. Can you see it?"

Mr Whyte looked up. The sun hurt his eyes.

"It's flying straight, Jason," he said. "I don't think it's looking for us."

"It's very high," said Jason. "I suppose it's a plane on its way to Miami. I thought it was looking for us!"

"We'll be found, son," said Jason's Papa. "Make no mistake about that. Your mother's a clever woman. Everyone will be out searching for us by now. I'll just say another prayer."

Jason heard his father praying again. The words sounded very simple and moving. William Whyte was asking God to take them home. Jason wanted to go home. He wanted to go home more than anything else. He believed what his father said—"No man is ever alone,"—but he wanted to go home.

7. Rough weather

Jason and his father woke from a light doze. Neither of them had been able to sleep properly through the dark night.

"Man, I've never felt so cold," said Mr Whyte, shivering in his thin shirt. "I wish we had something to cover ourselves with."

Jason hugged himself with his arms, and looked at the sky. There was a mass of black cloud across it, looking like a torn curtain, with patches of light grey cloud showing through the holes in the mass.

"Stormy weather today," said his father. "But the rain won't come till later. You must try for a fish, man. I'm so hungry I could eat the boat!"

Jason made tight the piece of white rag which he was using as bait on the end of the line. He dropped it into the dark grey sea. The sea was dark grey everywhere, except where a pink patch of cloud reflected itself on the surface. The cut-out shapes of the cloud changed all the time. The line felt limp in his hand. Somewhere, very high up, an aeroplane flew. Jason could hear it, but he could see nothing. He said nothing to Papa, who looked tired and old.

Jason held the line for a very long time. Nothing happened. His arm was beginning to ache, when he heard a steady, drumming sound, and looked across the water. A grey wall of rain was coming towards them.

"Rain," said Jason briefly. "Papa, get under the cover."

As the rain came nearer Jason noticed how slowly his father moved. He seemed to be dragging his legs. The sea was a flat sheet of steel, and the noise of the rain grew louder. Just before it hit the canoe it broke the water up with thousands of raindrops—they danced and hissed as the rain fell down. Jason was drenched to the skin in a moment. The rain poured into the boat, and its rushing noise became a loud roar.

Jason felt the canoe rock as the surface of the sea rose into waves. As he began to bail out water with the calabash, the wind rose, and the rain stopped. White crests appeared on the waves. The wind blew stronger, and the canoe bobbed up and down. Mr Whyte crawled from under the cover.

"I'll help to bail," he said. "But I have a fierce pain in my chest."

"The rain's stopped," said Jason. "You sit down and rest, Papa."

As Jason spoke, a huge wave hit the canoe. The foaming water rose high and came over them both.

"Bail out the water," shouted Jason's father. "Give me the other half of the calabash. We'll both bail."

The sea was almost black. Everything was dark, except for the bright, white tops of the waves. The canoe went down into deep troughs of water, and up to the crests. Jason bailed, and looked at his father. The old man's clothes were soaked through, and he seemed to be forcing his arms to move.

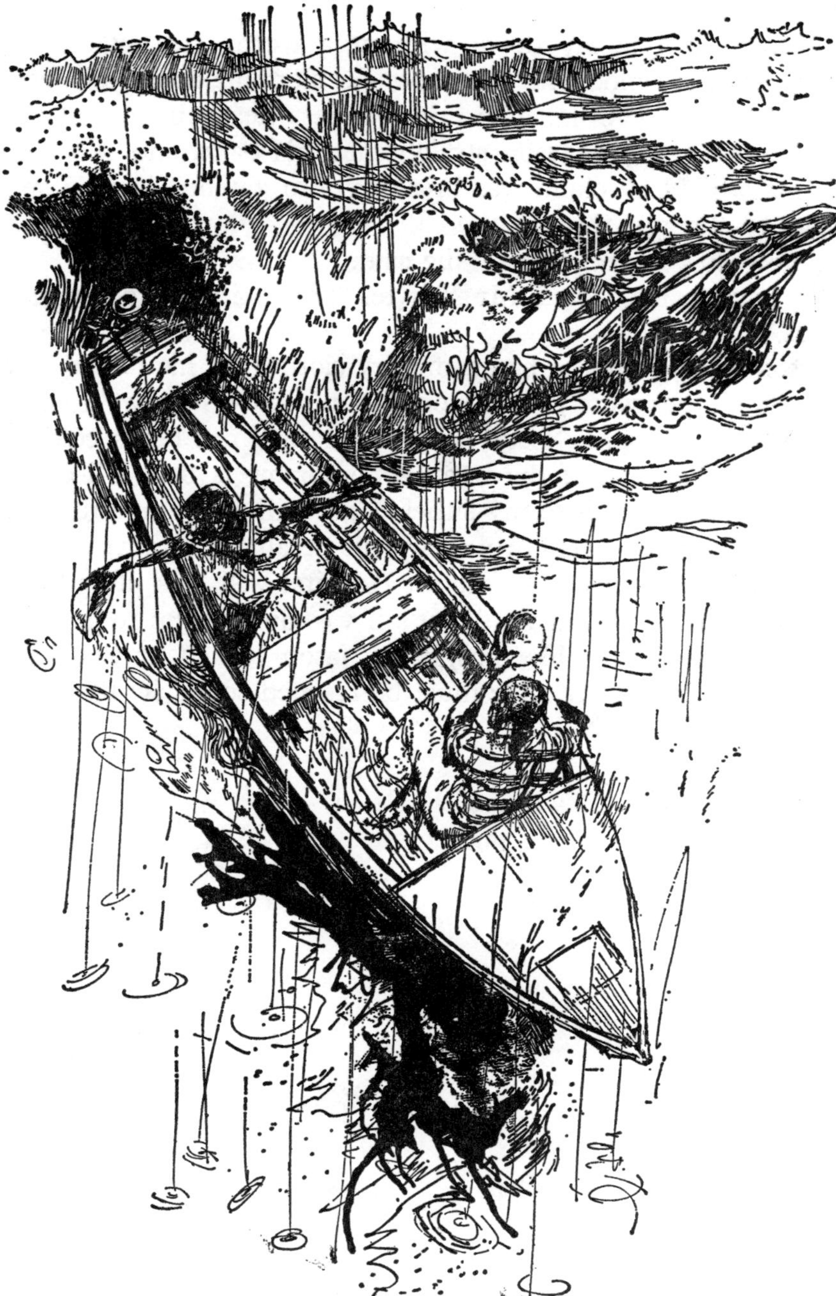

"Rest, Papa," he said. "Lie down on the spare boards."

William Whyte lay down without a word. He lay on the bottom of the canoe with the sea-water slopping round his legs. Jason went on bailing. The rain was less heavy now, and the wind was dropping. Jason straightened his back, and saw that the mass of black cloud was breaking into patches. A pale sun began to struggle through.

"How do you feel, Papa?" he said.

"I have pains," said Mr Whyte. "Pains in my chest and knees."

Jason wished that he had some dry clothes for his father, but his own clothes were just as wet. 'I don't know how we'll sleep tonight,' he thought. 'Let's hope that it will not be as cold as last night. Perhaps, if the weather tomorrow is fine, I'll catch a big fish, and feed it to my father. That will give him strength. If I can keep his strength up, he will be all right until we are rescued. The nurses at Falmouth Hospital will look after him. He will soon be well again. That's if we can get him to go into hospital—he doesn't like hospitals.' Jason looked at the still, wet form of his father. 'We must be rescued soon,' he thought.

8. Jason and a dolphin

It was already a fine day when Jason woke up. Mr Whyte was still sleeping in the bottom of the canoe. Jason tied the fishing line to the outboard motor. Then he took up the old paddle and dipped the blade over the side.

"I'll catch a dolphin today," he said aloud. "I'll feed my father today!"

There was fresh water in the cover of the motor. Jason had turned it upside down to catch the rain. Now he would save it for Papa to drink when he ate the fish.

The sun shone golden on the little waves. It was hard to think that there had been rough weather yesterday. But there was still no land in sight—only water everywhere.

"Come on, friend fish," said Jason. "I must catch you for my father."

William Whyte sat up slowly. He tried to smile at his son.

"A fine day, Jason," he said. "Cho, man, all these fish around us and you can't catch one! You catch one and I'll eat it, bones and all!"

Jason did not feel hungry any more, but felt he must make his father eat. He watched Papa take off his wet shirt and pants and lay them out in the sun to dry.

"You take the line in your hand, Papa," he said. "I'm tired of paddling. I'm going to get that motor going."

"I think I'll lie down and wait for my breakfast," said Mr Whyte. Jason could tell that he was not feeling well.

"You call me when breakfast is on the table," Mr Whyte said.

"Drink this rain-water first," said Jason. "I caught it yesterday."

His father did not seem thirsty. He drank only a sip, and then

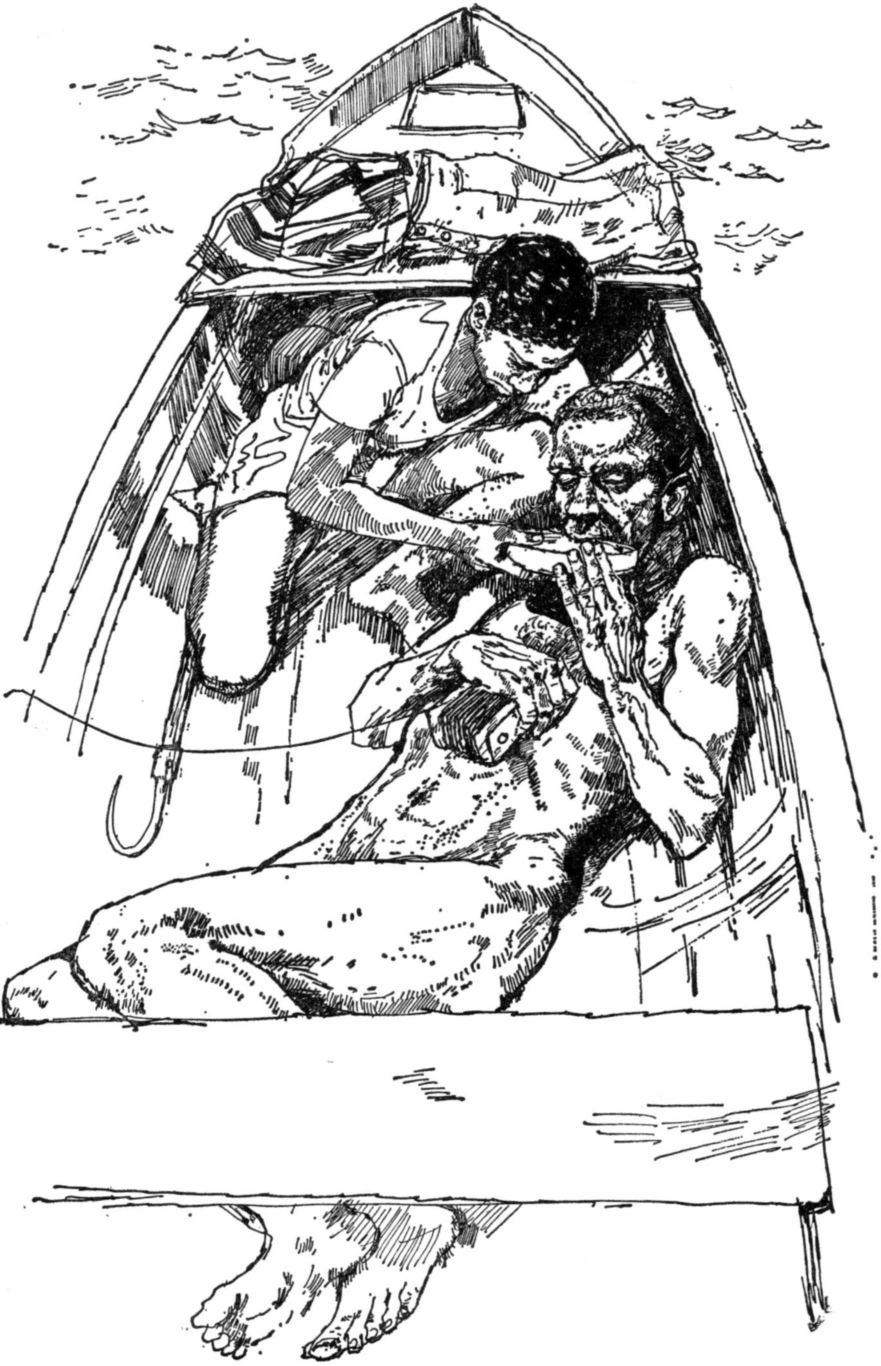

lay down on the boards. Jason took a little drink himself. It tasted so good!

He began to work on the engine again. He cleaned all the parts once more, and pulled and pulled the starting cord. Nothing happened. There was not even a spark.

Papa was praying again. Jason could hear the soft words in the deep, warm voice. Every few minutes Papa paused for a little while and then, after a few moments, started again.

Jason took the cover of the motor with the water in it, and knelt down to his father.

"Papa, drink," he said.

Mr Whyte sipped a little more of the water. Then he closed his eyes, and seemed to fall asleep. The fishing line was still in his hand.

Jason thought, 'Even a dolphin would be all right. I could get the skin off with my teeth and then chew the raw fish for him. It is very tough and tastes too sweet, but he would eat it.'

"Thank you, Father," said Mr Whyte softly. "Thank you for being with us on the sea. Thank you for being with all men everywhere."

Jason crouched down by him.

"Are you all right, Papa?" he asked. "Can I get you some more water?" He took the line and wound it round his own hand. "I shall catch a fish soon. I shall catch a fish for you."

"Jason!" said Mr Whyte. "Try to get home and take care of your mother."

There was a gentle pull on the line. Jason went to the bow of the canoe, and waited and waited. There was a harder pull. He could feel the weight of the fish. Jason let the line slip down through his fingers . . . more and more line. Then he began to pull . . . gently at first, then more strongly. The weight grew heavier. Jason felt for the gaff with his toes, and picked it up with his left hand. The fish was caught. It was coming up! 'Food for Papa,' thought Jason. 'Strength for Papa!'

"It will be a dolphin," Jason said aloud. "A dolphin with stripes and purple spots. A golden dolphin for Papa!"

He now changed the line to his left hand, and held the stick with the hook on it in his right hand. Suddenly the line jerked wildly, and a dolphin came leaping and twirling out of the sea. Jason moved to the stern of the canoe carefully, and began to haul the fish in. Then, quickly, he leaned over the stern and hooked it with the gaff.

"Papa," he panted, "Papa, here's a fish for your breakfast. Wake up, Papa. Wake up! Why don't you wake up?"

9. Jason alone

But Papa hadn't woken up, thought Jason. Papa had never woken up again. And now, all the days seemed the same.

"I'm on my own now," said Jason to himself. "Yet I don't feel alone. Papa was right. No man is ever alone. I kept Papa's body in the boat as long as I could, I really did!" He knew that he had counted up to twelve days after his father's death. Twelve days of sunshine after dark, silent nights. Twelve days of sheltering under the cover at the end of the canoe. Twelve cold, dark nights when the far-away lights of ships passed by.

"I can think of one special day," said Jason to the sea and the sky. "The day the shark came to see me."

Jason had caught about twelve dolphins after the first one. He had not even needed to trail the line behind the boat. The dolphins kept together, and it had been easy to catch them with the gaff. 'What a pity they had to die,' thought Jason. 'They are all the colours of the rainbow in the water, but they are so plain in the boat. I can't remember if I ate any. I think they tasted bad! I wonder if the shark thought that I had caught the dolphins for him.'

Jason had felt no fear as the shark cut through the blue water towards the canoe. He only felt interested in seeing the high fin moving so fast, just cutting the surface. 'The shark is my friend,' the boy thought. 'He has come to visit, to show me that I have a friend in the deep waters.' He watched as the long body of the shark came up through the water. The shark had yellow eyes and gills on each side of his head.

"What happened, friend?" said Jason.

The shark rubbed his flat snout against the canoe, and swam towards the bow with a side-to-side bending of his body. He was much longer than the canoe. He seemed to be looking at the lettering on it—WHAT'S THAT TO YOU?.

"Can you read, shark?" asked Jason. "Reading was my best subject at school."

The big fish began to swim slowly round and round Jason and the boat.

"Stay still," said Jason. "If you are my friend, you should stay still when you come to visit."

The shark came slowly round to the stern, and his head came out of the water. He looked at Jason with his strange eyes. Jason leaned over the side and put his hand on the shark's back. He rubbed the skin towards the tail, and it felt fairly smooth. It was very rough when he rubbed it the other way. The fish kept quite still while Jason stroked his skin, but when Jason stopped, he began to encircle the boat again, swimming just below the surface.

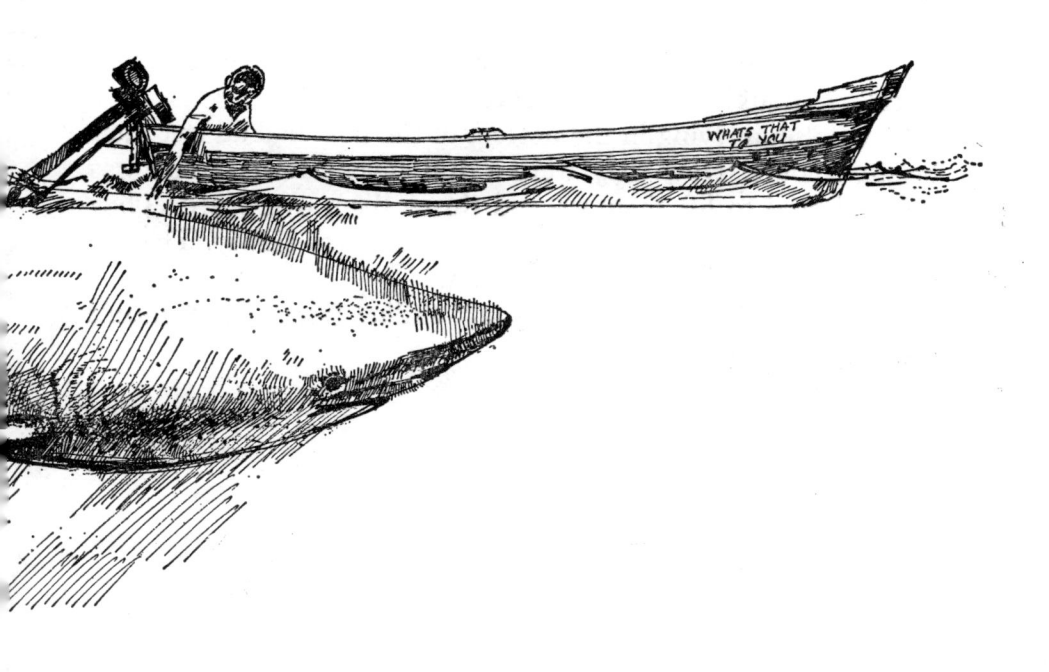

"I live on fish," said Jason to the shark. "And so do you."

'That was not quite true,' he thought then, 'but it will please my fish-friend to hear it! While I've been on the sea all these days I've thought of rice and peas, yams, roast beef with gravy, and sweet potatoes cooked all shiny in sugar. Some days I don't feel hungry at all, though. Sometimes I think that I couldn't eat anything. But I can always drink! The day it rained a little I caught some of it; and my throat felt so good, and not dry at all.'

"Are you hungry, fish?" he asked.

The shark raised his head high. The large mouth was closed, and he looked as if he were smiling! Jason smiled too.

"I remember my father used to say that if a fish like you came to call, I should give it the biggest fish I had."

The dolphins lying in the bottom of the boat had all lost their bright colours. Now they were a dull silver-brown. Jason was quite pleased to lift them up and throw them overboard. They floated for a moment, and then went down very slowly. The big shark dived deep in a flurry of foam.

"You could have said thank-you," smiled Jason. "You didn't even say goodbye!"

10. The Rescue

Day followed day, and Jason could not remember how many days had passed. After his friend the shark had left him, nothing seemed to happen. The nights were always dark and cold. The days were always bright and sunny. Aeroplanes passed high overhead during the day. Ships passed far away during the night. Jason drank a little rain-water from one brief shower. When that was finished, he drank a little sea-water. He swam close to the boat in the deep, blue, calm water. He longed to go home.

'The boat is getting very waterlogged,' he thought one day. 'I shall have to drop the outboard motor into the sea.' The motor seemed like his last link with shops, town, and people, as it splashed and sank.

"But I shall live," Jason said aloud. "I'm living now. I don't even feel hungry any more. Someone will see me. I know they will."

The golden sun had not been up very long. Jason looked at the sea, and the broad band of grey-blue sky above it. The clouds there changed to orange-pink, and he watched some big, white sea birds fly up through them and on into a green-blue patch beyond. Then they flew up behind some wisps of pink cloud and were gone.

"Friend Sun," said Jason, "you are climbing up like the birds. You will make me hide in the covered part of the boat."

The soles of Jason's feet were burnt from the heat of the wood. His palms hurt too. But, as he crouched in the shade of the cover, he did not think of his hands or feet. He thought of his carving.

'I miss my carving,' he thought. 'It would be very useful if I could carve in the boat. I should have so much work ready for the next bus-load of tourists.' He thought of the tourists with their new, shiny clothes, their sun-glasses and their cameras. They were always laughing and happy. 'They often say they love Jamaica,' Jason thought. 'And so do I.'

He came out from under the cover. 'I'll ask myself a few questions,' he thought. 'I'll be like a teacher at school.'

"Who are you?" he asked.

"I am Jason Whyte," he answered.

"How old are you?" he asked.

"I am fourteen years old," he answered.

"Where do you live?" he asked.

"I live in a district called Rock, in Trelawney," he answered.

"What is the name of your island?" he asked.

"Jamaica," Jason answered.

"Well done," said Jason to himself. "You may go for a long swim as a reward!"

He jumped into the clear water and swam until the sun stood directly above him in the sky. Then he climbed back into the canoe, shook the drops from his head, and looked around.

"A ship!" he shouted. "I can see a ship!"

'I wonder why I didn't see it before?' he thought. Then he said, "It's here. I can see people!"

Jason stood up in the canoe. He waved and waved. The ship was a freighter. He strained his eyes to see the name.

Eibe Oldendorff he read.

"It sounds like German," Jason said. "Hi, *Eibe Oldendorff*! Can you see me?"

The cargo ship came closer, and Jason waved to the people he could see on board. They waved back at him. Someone threw a rope. Jason jumped into the water and swam. Two seamen jumped from the ship and swam towards him. They held the rope, and helped him to climb up. Very soon he was on the deck. A group of men stood round him.

"Sprechen sie Deutsch?" said one man in careful German.

Jason said nothing. He felt completely dazed.

"Sit down. Have some coffee," said another man in English.

Jason drank the hot coffee. Nothing had ever tasted so fine.

The first seaman wrapped a blanket round his shoulders. The second man called for someone called 'Der Kapitan'.

"You speak English, no?" he asked.

"Yes," Jason said.

Jason found it hard to speak to anyone after all the days of being alone.

He had talked to himself all the time, but this was different. A man walked towards him on the deck. Jason thought that he must be the captain of the ship. He smiled at the boy.

"What is your name?" the captain asked.

"I am Jason Whyte," Jason answered.

"Where do you come from, Jason?" asked the captain.

"Jamaica," answered Jason, and he thought, 'It is just like the talk I had with myself in the boat.'

"How did you come to be in the open sea, nearly three hundred miles from your home, Jason?"

Jason took the food a seaman gave him and began to eat. It was strange to be eating after all this time. He didn't feel like talking.

"Did you go rowing on your own?"

Jason shook his head. The captain smiled kindly.

"Ach, I understand. You went fishing and drifted away from land?"

Jason nodded.

"Bring the boy's boat on deck," the captain ordered. "We are a cargo ship sailing from New Orleans to Panama, Jason. We will take you with us. There is a hospital in Panama where you can rest and get strong again. Do you know how many days you have been lost at sea?"

Jason shook his head.

"Anyway, you are safe now, Jason. There will be a Jamaican Consul in Panama. He will look after you, and return you to your family in Jamaica."

Suddenly Jason thought of Papa, and his eyes filled with tears. Then he heard Papa's voice in his mind. 'Take care of your mother,' the voice said. Jason smiled at the captain and the crew.

"I should like to go home," he said.

Questions

1

1 What have you learnt about Jason's home and family? In what ways is your home different?
2 Who was Jason's 'grown-up friend'? What is a cabinet-maker?
3 Why was Jason disappointed when his mother told him he was going fishing? What would he rather have done instead?

2

1 What was the name of Mr Whyte's boat? What name would you choose for a boat and why?
2 Where did Jason's father work when he was a young man? What kind of work does he do now?
3 Did you recognise any of the fish that Jason hoped to catch? Make a list of some others that you have seen.

3

1 Why did Mr Whyte decide to turn back home before his friends? Do you think Jason wanted to go home?
2 What did Mr Whyte mean when he described his wife as ". . . a good woman; no fussing with her".
3 Can you explain why the men in the other boat did not answer Jason's call?

4

1 How did Jason and his father propel the boat after the engine had failed?
2 Explain what Jason's father meant when he said, "I'll take the first turn".
3 What is the 'shelf' that goes around the island of Jamaica?
4 Why did Jason think it would help if he was a sea bird?

5

1 What had happened to the boat while Jason and his father slept?

2 Why was Jason pleased to see the brown and white bird?
3 How did Jason's father think they might be rescued?

6

1 What made Jason think that an aeroplane might not see the small boat?
2 What did Jason's father mean when he said, "No man is ever alone"?
3 Jason swam around the boat to keep cool. Make a list of the ways that you know of keeping cool on a hot day.

7

1 'Jason made tight the piece of white rag . . .' What does this mean?
2 What happened during the storm when the wind rose?
3 How did Jason think he could give his father strength until they were rescued?
4 Why do you think Mr Whyte would not want to go to a hospital?

8

1 How had Jason managed to collect drinking water?
2 How did Jason know that his father was not feeling well?
3 Can you describe how Jason managed at last to catch a fish?

9

1 How many days had gone by since Jason's father died? How did Jason spend this time on his own?
2 Why was Jason pleased to see the shark?
3 Why do you think Jason's father had told Jason always to feed a shark with the biggest fish he had?

10

1 Why did Jason throw the outboard motor into the sea?
2 What kind of ship finally rescued Jason? What country did it belong to?
3 Describe how Jason reached the ship.
4 Where did the sailors take Jason? Can you think of a reason why he did not go straight back to Jamaica?

Glossary

1

to carve to make a shape by cutting wood or stone
cabinet-maker person who makes furniture
rooster domestic cock
mangrove tropical tree which grows in salt-water swamps and sends down new roots from its branches
swamp soft, wet land
marl mixture of clay and lime, used to reclaim swamp land
to hug to hold tightly with the arms
garbage can bin for waste food
kerosene paraffin
verandah roofed and floored open space along the side of a building
plantain kinds of large banana
gas gasolene; petrol
outboard motor motor attached to the back of a boat

2

paddle short oar with a broad blade at one end
gaff stick with an iron hook used for landing fish
dolphin sea animal like a very small whale
to trail to pull along behind
conch shell large spiral shell
to chug to make the short explosive sound of a petrol-engine running slowly
wrought iron iron shaped by hammering while hot
canoe long, narrow boat
to bob to make a quick, short, down-and-up movement
chuckle low, quiet laugh
haul amount of fish caught in a net
splutter sound as if spitting

3

Portuguese man-o'-war sea animal with a sail-like crest which floats on the surface

tentacles long, slender, boneless part of certain animals used for feeding, holding etc.
coral hard, red, pink or white substance built up on the sea-bed by small sea-creatures, forming reefs and islands when it reaches the surface
to dart to move forward suddenly and quickly
flying fish fish which rises in the air with the help of fins
stern back end of a ship or boat
gnarled rough and twisted
fussing unnecessary worrying, especially about unimportant things
carburettor part of an engine
to lap (of water) to move gently against something
to heave to rise and fall
swell slow rise and fall of the sea's surface

4

to paddle to send a boat through the water by using one or two paddles
land breeze a soft, gentle wind blowing from the land at certain hours
westward current stream of water flowing towards the west
to swirl to move or flow round
to drift to be carried along by a current of air or water
to droop to bend or hang down because of tiredness or weakness
lagoon salt-water lake separated from the sea by sandbanks
to shimmer to shine with a soft light
to glisten to shine

5

to mumble to speak indistinctly
bow front end of a boat or ship
surf waves breaking in white foam on the sea-shore
bait food put on a hook to catch fish
motor-launch passenger-carrying boat driven by petrol or electricity
helicopter aircraft with rotating blades on top

6

to spot to pick out one person or thing out of many
to crouch to stoop with arms and legs together
to scramble to climb or crawl
to doze to sleep lightly; be half asleep
to drench to wet all over, right through
foam white mass of small bubbles
to bail to throw water out of a boat
calabash hard, outer skin or shell of a gourd, used for holding liquids

trough (of the sea) long hollow between two waves
crest white top edge of a wave
to soak to make very wet
to slop (of liquids) to spill over the edge of something

8

to chew to work food about between the teeth in order to crush it
to twirl to move round and round

9

shark large sea-fish that eats other fish
fin (see drawing)
gill opening (see drawing)
snout animal's nose and mouth
flurry short, sudden rush

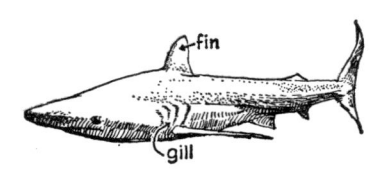

10

waterlogged so soaked with water that it will barely float
wisp small piece (of smoke, cloud, etc.)
freighter cargo ship
to strain to try very hard
Sprechen sie Deutsch? Do you speak German?
dazed stupid; unable to think clearly
der Kapitan the captain
Consul State's agent living in a foreign town to help and protect his countrymen there

Oxford University Press, Ely House, London W. 1
GLASGOW NEW YORK TORONTO MELBOURNE WELLINGTON
CAPE TOWN IBADAN NAIROBI DAR ES SALAAM LUSAKA ADDIS ABABA
DELHI BOMBAY CALCUTTA MADRAS KARACHI LAHORE DACCA
KUALA LUMPUR SINGAPORE HONG KONG TOKYO

ISBN 0 19 422675 1
© *Oxford University Press 1973*

Printed in Great Britain by
Hazell, Watson and Viney Ltd
Aylesbury, Bucks.